Casper Jaggi

Other Badger Biographies

Casper Jaggi

Master Swiss Cheese Maker

JERRY APPS

WISCONSIN HISTORICAL SOCIETY PRESS

Published by the Wisconsin Historical Society Press
Publishers since 1855

© 2008 by State Historical Society of Wisconsin

Publication of this book was made possible, in part, by a gift from Mrs. Harvey E. Vick of Milwaukee, Wisconsin.

wisconsinhistory.org

All images are courtesy of the Wisconsin Historical Society unless otherwise indicated. Photographs identified with WHi are from the Society's collections; address inquiries about these photos to the Visual Materials Archivist at the Wisconsin Historical Society, 816 State Street, Madison, Wisconsin, 53706.

Printed in the United States of America
Designed by Emily Korsmo

13 12 11 10 09   2 3 4 5 6

Front cover: Casper Jaggi and his wheels of Swiss cheese, Wisconsin Historical Society, WHi Image ID 33258. Back cover: Photo of a Brown Swiss cow, courtesy of the Wisconsin Milk Marketing Board Inc.

Apps, Jerold W., 1934–
    Casper Jaggi : master Swiss cheese maker / Jerry Apps.
        p. cm.—(Badger biographies)
    Includes bibliographical references and index.
    ISBN 978-0-87020-392-3 (pbk. : alk. paper) 1. Jaggi, Casper, 1893–1971—Juvenile literature. 2. Cheesemakers—Wisconsin—Green County—Biography—Juvenile literature. 3. Swiss cheese—History—Juvenile literature. I. Title.
    SF272.S9.A77 2008
    637'.3092—dc22
    [B]
                            2007037325

To the untiring generations of Wisconsin cheese makers who continue to produce the best cheese in the world and to the dairy farmers who provide the tons of milk necessary for making the billions of pounds of cheese Wisconsin produces each year.

Contents

1

Meet Casper Jaggi

America's Dairyland. Those two words on Wisconsin license plates tell you a lot about the state and its agricultural **heritage**. As you drive along country roads in Wisconsin, you'll see barns and cows grazing in fields nearby. Some of their milk becomes something you drink. Some of the milk is used to make cheese.

A Wisconsin license plate

heritage (**her** uh tij): traditions and culture passed on by ancestors

Many European **immigrants** who settled in Wisconsin more than 100 years ago brought their cheese-making traditions with them. One of them was **Casper Jaggi**, who

came from Switzerland and moved to Green County. To this day, that part of the state is famous for its cheese.

Casper became an **expert** at making Swiss cheese and produced a lot of it. He eventually owned the largest Swiss cheese factory in Wisconsin in the 1950s.

Casper Jaggi in his Brodhead Swiss Cheese Factory with Kenneth Clark (wearing the hat), one of his workers.

immigrant (**im** uh gruhnt): someone who leaves a country to permanently live in another country
Casper Jaggi (**kas** pur **yah** gee)
expert: someone who knows a lot about a topic

2

This is the story of an **entrepreneur** who started a company doing something he loved. But cheese making was more than a business for Casper. It was an **art**. It also continued a family tradition. When he was a little boy, Casper learned about cheese making from his father. Casper later passed these skills on to his son, Fritz, when Fritz also was just a young boy.

Casper Jaggi is an example of the many immigrant cheese makers who came to Wisconsin with special skills and contributed greatly to the state's agricultural history. He and others like him set the pace for the **master** cheese makers in Wisconsin today.

entrepreneur (ahn truh preh **nur**): person who starts his or her business from scratch
art: a skill gained after much practice and study
master: an expert

2

Casper's Swiss Traditions Find a New Home

Casper Jaggi was born in Europe on August 13, 1893, in Nessenthal, **Canton** Bern, Switzerland. Back then, Canton Bern was well known for its cheese, especially Swiss cheese. Even today, Swiss cheese making is common in Canton Bern.

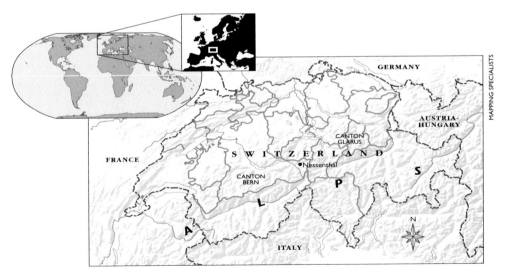

Switzerland's cantons in 1893. Casper came from Canton Bern.

canton: one of the states of Switzerland

IMAGE ENVISION

A scene from the Swiss Alps. Casper used milk from his family's cows when he first made cheese in the mountains.

Casper was just 6 years old when his father started teaching him the many steps involved in making cheese. Each spring, when the snow melted in the **highlands** of the Swiss Alps, young Casper and his father **drove** their cattle into the mountains to graze on the lush pastures. They spent summers up there, caring for their cows and making cheese from the milk. They had no electricity and worked by the light of a lantern or candlelight in the evenings. The water they needed came from streams and waterfalls. The Jaggis burned wood or coal to heat the kettles used to make their Swiss cheese. When Casper was little, he had to stand on a tree stump so he could look into the kettle!

highland: an area with mountains or hills
drove: moved something in a certain direction

In early fall, winter winds and snow began threatening. That's when the Jaggis drove their cattle back down to the valley where they spent the long winter. Casper and his father patiently waited for spring and the green grass. Then they could once more return their cattle to the high country.

Casper's mother died when he was very young, leaving his father to raise him. Casper helped his father with the cows and with cheese making for several years. His father taught him that Swiss cheese should taste like a green nut when it's in the kettle. Later, when it was aged, it should taste like a ripe nut. As Casper grew older, he **sharpened** his skills as a cheese maker. But Casper learned about cheese making one skill at a time.

First, he was taught how important it was to have clean equipment. If his father thought he hadn't cleaned one thing properly, he'd make Casper start over and wash everything again. "If you can't do a job right, don't do it at all," his father told him. Casper would never forget those words of advice.

sharpened: improved

COLLECTION OF FRITZ AND DONNA JAGGI

Casper (center) and his brothers Andrew and John at Andrew's farm near New Glarus, Wisconsin

Casper was the youngest of 4 boys. His older brothers, Andrew and John, left Switzerland for the United States when Casper was a teenager. Andrew and John lived on farms in Green County, Wisconsin, near New Glarus. This community is located about 20 miles southwest of Madison. It had been established in 1845 by Nicholas Durst and **Fridolin Steiff** from Canton Glarus in Switzerland.

Fridolin Steiff (**free** do lin **stife**)

Durst and Steiff had come to southern Wisconsin in search of land for themselves and for other people from Switzerland. At the time, people living in Canton Glarus were very poor and were looking for a place where they could make a better life. Durst and Steiff bought 1,280 **acres** near present-day New Glarus. This land would be shared by more than 100 other Swiss immigrants from their canton who would soon arrive. Then more people from other parts of Switzerland followed. Casper's brothers moved to New Glarus because Swiss settlers from their home in Canton Bern had already immigrated there. Andrew and John knew they would be comfortable among people from their homeland. They all spoke the same language and shared many of the same traditions.

By the time he was in his late teens, Casper wanted to follow his brothers to the United States. In 1913, when he was 20, he joined them in New Glarus.

acre (**ay** kur): a measurement of area that is almost the size of a football field

Swiss in Wisconsin

The first Swiss immigrants came to Wisconsin in the mid-1820s, before Wisconsin had even become a state. They settled in southwestern Wisconsin, near the villages of Shullsburg and **Gratiot**. By 1890, people of Swiss heritage were found in nearly every Wisconsin county. By 1900, about 12,000 Swiss had settled in Wisconsin.

The Midwestern United States was **appealing** to Swiss immigrants because the land was **inexpensive**.

The first Swiss saw southern Wisconsin's rich soils. Even though

Many of the first Swiss to immigrate to Wisconsin settled in the southwestern part of the state.

they found no mountains, the gentle hills reminded them a bit of Switzerland. Farming became the main occupation for these immigrants. Like other pioneers in the area, they plowed the rolling land. They then planted fields of wheat.

Gratiot (**gra** shut)
appealing: pleasing and of interest
inexpensive: reasonable in price

9

But planting wheat in the same ground year after year soon used up the soil's **nutrients**. It became harder to grow wheat on this land. Cows and dairy farming replaced many of these wheat fields.

Several of the Swiss settlers who made their farms in Green County, Wisconsin, eventually started to use the cheese-making skills they brought from Switzerland. People thought that the cheese they made in Wisconsin tasted good enough to be compared with cheese from Switzerland. According to a local newspaper article from 1915, "[P]eople in the large cities became aware that cheese made in Green county was nearly, if not wholly, as good as the **imported** article."

"Honey Belle," a painted cow in front of the Historic Cheesemaking Center in Monroe, Wisconsin. Some Green County residents wear traditional Swiss clothing at festivals celebrating their heritage.

Today, the city of Monroe in Green County calls itself the Swiss Cheese Capital of the U.S.A. Every other September, they host Cheese Days. People can sample different cheeses, watch cheese-making **demonstrations**, and tour a cheese factory. Everyone is encouraged to wear traditional Swiss clothing. New Glarus also continues to celebrate its Swiss heritage at festivals each year.

nutrient (**noo** tree uhnt): something that is needed to stay healthy
imported: brought into a country from another place or region
demonstration: a display of how something is done

10

3

The Making of a Swiss Cheese Maker

When Casper arrived in New Glarus, he found a landscape very different from the Swiss Alps of his homeland. The area of Green County around New Glarus was hilly instead of mountainous. But the important thing was that the open fields were green in summer.

WHI IMAGE ID 42587

This photograph of New Glarus was taken around 1910. It shows what the area looked like a few years before Casper settled there.

Casper began working with his brothers, clearing land for farming. He was amazed by the size of the farms in Green County. In Switzerland, farms were tiny, with steep fields that made them difficult to **till**. Many of the farms in and around New Glarus were 80 or often 160 acres, more than 8 to 10 times bigger than a typical Swiss farm. Even better, because the hills were not as steep as the Swiss mountains Casper remembered, nearly all of the land could be tilled. More land also meant that crops such as corn and other vegetables could be planted and harvested.

But Casper quickly discovered that he missed making cheese. He realized he'd rather make cheese than do farmwork. Soon he was helping wash cheese in nearby Swiss cheese factories around Green County.

It is important to "wash" Swiss cheese because various **molds** develop on the outside of the cheese as it is **cured**. Casper and other workers washed cheese by regularly rubbing salty **whey** over the Swiss cheese wheels.

till: to prepare land for growing crops
mold: a fungus that grows on old food or damp surfaces
cured (**kyurd**): prepared for use
whey (**way**): the watery part of milk that separates in sour milk or when you make cheese

What's Whey?

Whey is a watery **by-product** of making cheese. For many years, whey was a problem for cheese makers such as Casper. They didn't know what to do with it. Some cheese makers dumped the whey into rivers and streams. Some spread it on farmers' fields.

Many farmers who delivered milk to Casper's cheese factory also raised pigs. Casper's milk haulers returned whey to those farmers. They, in turn, fed the whey to their pigs. Casper's milk trucks had space to haul milk cans and a tank to hold gallons of whey. When the milk truck arrived at a farm, the farmer could drain off some whey for his or her pigs.

Today, whey is used in many ways besides food for pigs. It's used in bakery products, energy bars, and infant formulas. Researchers are also looking for nonfood uses of whey. For example, researchers in California are studying whether whey can be used to make **edible** food containers. Whey is no longer a useless by-product of cheese making. It's now a valuable product in its own right.

by-product: something that is left over after you make or do something
edible (**ed** uh buhl): able to be eaten

13

Washing cheese was hard work. It meant lifting and turning heavy, round wheels of cheese, some weighing as much as 200 pounds! Casper earned money for several years as a hired man in cheese factories around New Glarus.

Casper's future wife, Frieda Fuhrer, on a steamship crossing the Atlantic Ocean. She also left Switzerland to make a new life in the United States.

When he had free time, Casper often visited Monroe, a town also home to many Swiss immigrants. One day in 1920, he met a beautiful young woman named **Frieda Fuhrer**. She worked there in Mrs. Engles's candy and antiques store. Frieda had come to the United States from Switzerland. She had stayed with cousins in a Swiss community in Indiana before moving to Wisconsin. Casper and Frieda started meeting regularly at the shop and soon became a couple. On February 21, 1921, they were married.

Frieda Fuhrer (free da **fur** her)

Frieda and Casper on their wedding day in 1921. Standing behind them are Casper's brother Andrew and his wife, Marie.

14

Around this time, Casper was working in a Green County cheese factory near Albany. Frieda helped out at the factory, too. She did just about everything! She filled the kettles and washed the cheese.

A few years later, in 1923, Casper and Frieda moved to northeastern Wisconsin so that Casper could go to work for Kraft Foods company in Antigo. Casper became even more skilled at cheese making. But he was working in an old and drafty building. He knew that just a 2-degree difference in temperature could change the quality of the cheese.

Casper worked in cheese factories in each of these towns in Green County. He moved north to work in Antigo, but returned to southern Wisconsin after a year.

Casper's wife, Frieda, helped make cheese in copper kettles. This picture was taken in the early 1920s.

15

Casper became **frustrated** because he was not able to control the temperature in the cheese factory. After 1 year, the Jaggis returned to Green County. Casper made cheese for a year at County Line Factory near Albany.

For the next 15 years, from 1925 to 1940, Casper worked as a cheese maker for the Coldren Cheese Factory near Brodhead in Green County. This was a **cooperative** factory. The farmers who delivered milk to the Coldren Cheese Factory owned the business, and Casper worked for them.

Casper (at left) and other workers at the Coldren Cheese Factory near Brodhead. Each kettle produced one wheel of Swiss cheese.

frustrated: to feel helpless and discouraged
cooperative (koh **op** ur uh tiv): a business owned by all the people who work in it or are members of it

Casper (in overalls) with members of the Coldren Cheese Factory cooperative. He and Frieda lived in an apartment on the second floor.

But Casper owned the cheese-making equipment, so he earned a **percentage** of the money the factory took in from selling its cheese. He and Frieda moved into an apartment right above the factory.

percentage (pur **sen** tij): a portion of the whole amount

Got Milk—and Cheese?

How is milk different from cheese? Everyone knows the answer to that. You drink milk, and you eat cheese. Milk is 89 percent water. Cheese is 42 percent water. That's why you drink milk and eat cheese.

Cheese is made from milk. It takes 10 pounds of milk to make just one pound of cheese!

Milk and cheese are good for you. They contain fat, minerals, and protein. Milk and cheese also have lots of calcium, which is needed for strong bones. One **ounce** of natural Swiss cheese, like the kind Casper made, provides about 270 **milligrams** of calcium. A glass of low-fat milk has about 300 milligrams of calcium.

Young boys and girls need approximately 1,000 milligrams of calcium each day. So if you drink a glass of low-fat milk and eat a small piece of Swiss cheese daily, you will have more than half the calcium you need to build healthy bones!

ounce: a unit of weight equal to 1/16 of a pound
milligram: a unit of measurement in the metric system

Okay, so how does milk become cheese? Have you heard the nursery rhyme "Little Miss Muffet"? It goes like this: "Little Miss Muffet sat on her **tuffet** eating her **curds** and whey." Do you know what she was eating? She was eating freshly made cheese similar to cottage cheese. When cheese is made, milk is separated into curds and whey. Curds are really small hunks of cheese. And you already know about the watery whey. Separating curds from whey is one step in the cheese-making process.

While Casper was working at the Coldren Cheese Factory in 1938, he and Frieda adopted their son, Fritz. At the time, Fritz was 18 months old. Five years later Casper and Frieda adopted their daughter, Annabelle, when she was 6 months old. Fritz enjoyed being around the cheese factory, especially when his family lived right upstairs. He liked seeing the hard-working men and the equipment.

Frieda and Casper outside the Coldren Cheese Factory in 1938 with their newly adopted son, Fritz.

tuffet: a low seat or stool
curd (kurd): the solid part of sour milk that is used to make cheese

Annabelle didn't enjoy anything about cheese making, however. She rarely went inside the factory.

In 1941, Casper bought his own cheese factory. It was also located in Green County, in the town of Brodhead. He called it the Brodhead Swiss Cheese Factory. By the 1950s, it was the largest Swiss cheese factory in Wisconsin. It was a modern **plant** with 18 big copper kettles for making Swiss cheese. Casper had 12 to 14 **employees**. Many of them were also Swiss. Together, they made 26 wheels of Swiss cheese every day in the summer. Summer was the busiest time in the factory. That's when cows were feeding on grass and producing more milk.

The milk for Casper's cheese came from local farmers. Casper paid them based on the number of pounds of milk they sent to the factory and the butterfat content of the milk. Cheese makers wanted milk with more butterfat because it would **yield** greater amounts of cheese than milk with a lower amount of butterfat.

plant: a factory where a particular product is made
employee: someone who works for another and receives a salary from that person or business
yield (**yeeld**): to produce something

Testing Milk for Its Butterfat Content

Each farmer's milk was sampled and tested almost every day for its butterfat content. The higher the amount of butterfat, the more money the farmer received.

The amount of butterfat generally depended on the breed of cow giving the milk. For example, milk from a Jersey cow can have 5.5 percent butterfat, while milk from a Holstein cow might have only 3 percent butterfat. And butterfat content changes throughout the year for the same breed, depending on what a cow is eating. When a cow is fed a dry

The butterfat content of a cow's milk varies from breed to breed. A Guernsey, a cow with a reddish-brown coat, is pictured on the left. A black-and-white Holstein is on the right.

feed such as hay, the butterfat content of its milk will be higher than when it is **grazing** out in the pasture in the summer.

grazing: feeding on grass growing in a field

Some of Casper's cheese was sold at a shop located right in his Brodhead Swiss Cheese Factory. He also trucked it to Monroe and nearby Monticello. But most of his Swiss cheese was bought by a **wholesaler**. The wholesaler then sold Casper's cheese in Chicago.

The wholesaler sent one or two workers once a week in summer and once or twice a month in winter to pick up the cheese. They'd take the train from Chicago to Brodhead. When the train stopped, a railcar would be sent down a **spur** that headed from the main track right to the doors of Casper's factory! The workers would spend the day loading cheese onto the railcar. Remember that cows give more milk in the summer? For a cheese maker, more milk equals more cheese. So, in summer, the wholesaler's workers might have to stay overnight so they could fill another railcar with Casper's cheese the next day.

Casper was always coming up with ways to save time and have cheese making be less **strenuous** on his workers.

wholesaler: someone who buys large amounts of a product at a lower price in order to resell it at a higher price
spur: a railroad track that branches off from the main line
strenuous (**stren** yoo uhss): needing great effort

WHI IMAGE ID 33251

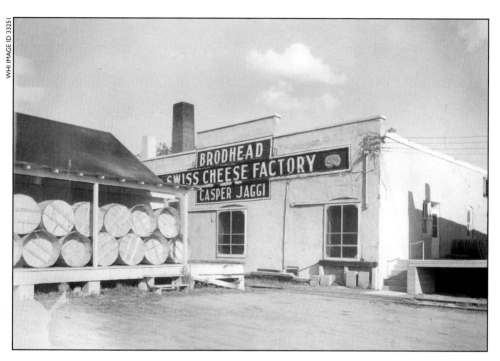

A spur off the main railroad track led right up to the back of Casper's Brodhead Swiss Cheese Factory. Can you find the tracks in this photo?

Cheese needed to be stirred constantly to keep it from burning. This work could be tiring, so Casper helped design a mechanical stirrer and a mechanical **cheese harp**. He also used a car part from a Model T to **mechanize** production in his factory.

cheese harp: a tool with a wooden frame and thin wires that is used to cut curds of cheese
mechanize (meh ka nize): to use machinery to replace human or animal labor

23

But Casper was more than just a skilled and **innovative** cheese maker. He was also a good **manager**, and this talent contributed to his success as a businessman. He knew how to work with other people and how to get the best from them.

Casper was never harsh with his employees and was always concerned about them and their families. He knew that to make good cheese, he had to keep his workers happy. He also knew how to get along with the farmers whose milk he bought. He understood that to receive quality milk, he needed to keep the farmers happy, too. Sometimes Casper would help a farmer make hay or cut wood.

Much of Casper's success was due to his "people skills." But without a good product, all the people skills in the world made no difference. Casper's business did well because of his ability to produce outstanding Swiss cheese. Customers bought his cheese because they thought it was delicious. Someone even ordered Casper's Swiss cheese from Korea, halfway around the world from Wisconsin. The postage to mail it cost more than the cheese!

innovative: known for new ideas or new inventions
manager: person in charge of a business or other employees at work

4

How Does Milk Become Cheese?

Every morning, 7 days a week, Casper's milk haulers drove his 6 trucks from farm to farm. Milk is **perishable**, so it had to be delivered quickly. That way, it wouldn't go bad before being turned into cheese.

At each farm, the milk haulers picked up 10-gallon cans of fresh milk from the farmer's cooling tank. A cooling tank was usually a water tank where fresh water flowed freely around the cans. Some farmers had just one or 2 cans. Others might have 8 or as many as 35 cans. The number of cans of milk a farmer had depended on how many cows he or she owned.

Some farmers brought their milk to the factory in their own trucks. One farmer delivered her milk by 6:00 a.m. She was indeed an early bird.

perishable (**per** ish uh buhl): likely to spoil or decay

WHI IMAGE ID 33395

One of Casper's workers dumped a 10-gallon can of milk into the scale tank at the left. He then placed the can on the **conveyor belt** at the right to be sent to a machine where it was washed.

When a milk truck arrived at Casper's Brodhead Swiss Cheese Factory, a worker dumped the milk from the cans into the scale tank that held 1,000 pounds of milk. From there the milk went to the scale dump. It next went to the holding tank. When the holding tank had 2,000 pounds of milk, there was enough to fill one kettle. That's when the milk was pumped through pipes running overhead.

Another worker ran the milk through a **cream separator** that took out some of the cream. Cream contains most of the butterfat in milk. You already learned that milk from different breeds of dairy cows differs in butterfat content. Milk for Swiss cheese making should have about 3.2 percent butterfat to keep the cheese at the right **consistency**. Too much butterfat would make the cheese greasy or sticky. Casper and

cream separator: a machine for separating cream from milk
consistency (kuhn **siss** tuhn see): degree of firmness
conveyor belt (kuhn **vay** ur belt): a moving belt that brings items to different places in a factory

Another worker watched as the separator removed some of the cream from the milk. Do you see the cream flowing into the pail?

This worker uses his left hand to help him measure when enough milk has been pumped into the kettle. He knew it was full when it reached his fingertips.

his workers usually removed one pail of cream from each batch of milk to get to the perfect 3.2 percent. Casper bottled some of the extra cream and sold it. He also sent some to a nearby creamery to be made into butter.

Once it came out of the cream separator, the milk was pumped through pipes into a round copper kettle. A Swiss cheese kettle was usually 6 feet in **diameter** and could hold about 2,000 pounds of milk! Some Swiss cheese makers claimed that the round copper kettles helped give Swiss cheese its nutty flavor. These big copper kettles became **symbols** of Swiss cheese making.

diameter: a straight line from one side of a circle, through the center, and to the other side
symbol: a design or object that is a representation of something else

WHI IMAGE ID 33264

The pole from the ceiling down into the middle of the kettle is the mechanical stirrer that Casper helped design. This worker is checking the temperature of the milk.

Next, Casper added a special **culture** called *Streptococcus lactis* and **rennet** to the milk in the kettle as it was being heated. For many years, the rennet used in cheese making came from the stomachs of milk-fed calves. Today it is made in laboratories. The rennet caused curd to form in the kettle. Casper then turned on his mechanized stirrer to help the curd separate from the whey.

culture (**kuhl** chur): a living material grown in a prepared medium
rennet (**re** nuht): an enzyme, or complex protein, added to milk to cause it to start changing from a liquid to a solid form

Good Bacteria

We often think that all **bacteria** are bad. Some do cause disease. But good bacteria exist, too. For example, the bacteria used in cheese making are good bacteria. One is *Streptococcus lactis*, a bacteria that changes **lactose** into lactic acid, which is a key part of the cheese making.

Cheese makers work hard to prevent the growth of harmful, disease-producing bacteria. To do this, they carefully control the temperature of the milk as it cooks. They also control the **acidity** as the cheese curds form. Remember Casper's first job as a child? The cheese maker also has to make sure that the cheese factory is kept spotlessly clean. The cheese maker does not want harmful bacteria to form.

When the curd became firm, workers used a curd cutter called a Swiss cheese harp to cut it into small cubes. The tool consisted of a wooden frame with thin wires that did the cutting. First, workers moved the cutter from back to front and side to side in the kettle. Then they stirred the curds for 15 to 30 minutes.

bacteria (bak **teer** ee uh): microscopic living things all around you and inside you
lactose (lak **tos**): a sugar that is present in milk
acidity (ah **si** duh tee): the amount of acid and sourness something contains

29

COLLECTION OF FRITZ AND DONNA JAGGI

Next, Casper and his workers heated the curds to about 120 to 130 degrees. They kept stirring for another 30 to 60 minutes until most of the curd was at the bottom of the kettle and the whey was floating on top. Can you imagine stirring 2,000 pounds of milk for an hour? Plus, the air temperature in the cheese factory often reached 110 degrees. Without air-conditioning, this was very hot and tiring work.

A Swiss cheese harp

At this step in the process, one of Casper's workers had to put his hands into the 120-degree kettle. He needed to place a loosely woven cloth called a "dipping cloth" under the curd. Some workers put their hands in cold water before plunging them into the hot curds and whey mixture.

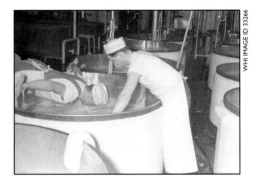

WHI IMAGE ID 33266

Does this look too close for comfort? These workers put their hands and arms into a kettle that was about 120 degrees. For a comparison, hot water coming out of your kitchen faucet is 120 degrees at its hottest. Most of us cannot keep our fingers under such hot water.

WHI IMAGE ID 33265

A worker leans over a kettle to tuck a cloth under the newly formed cheese curds. The T-bar holds his feet so he won't fall into the kettle of hot curds and whey.

To put the cloth in place, a worker leaned far over the edge of the wide copper kettle. Sometimes another worker held the man's feet so he wouldn't wind up in the kettle! Others put their feet under a specially made T-bar that kept them from falling in. Workers needed to repeat this step to recover the 4 or 5 pounds of curds they usually missed the first time.

31

WHI IMAGE ID 33267

A team of workers then tied the dipping cloth into a knot to make a bag, so the curds could be removed from the kettle.

With a special device called a block and tackle, workers
lifted the cloth containing the cheese curds out of the kettle.

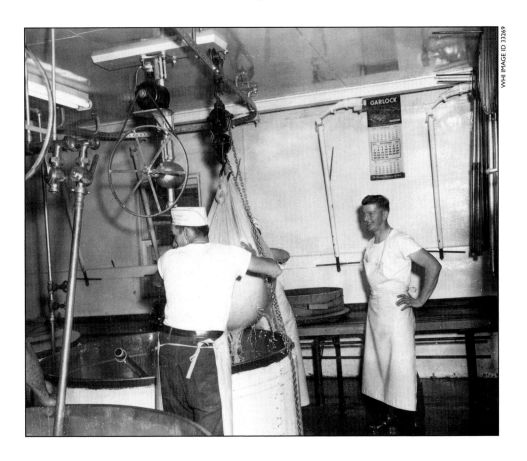

WHI IMAGE ID 33269

A worker had to hold the bag of curds above the kettle for a few minutes to let the excess whey drain back into the kettle. The workers squeezed the bag to help remove this liquid.

When most of the whey had drained out of the bag,
Casper and his workers pulled the bag of curds along the
overhead tracks to the press table.

WHI IMAGE ID 33282

Casper and one of his workers emptied the curd from the
dipping cloth into a round wooden **form** lined with material
called cheesecloth.

form: a frame or mold that will give something a particular shape

Workers covered the cheese with a special lid called a press lid. This lid was made of wood and was 2 inches thick. A machine gently pressed the cheese by pushing on the lid. The pressure forced more whey out of the cheese. That liquid drained out the bottom of the cheese form.

Casper presses the cheese curds to remove more whey. The liquid runs off the table, where it's collected in a stainless-steel tub. Casper had other uses for this extra whey.

After about 2 hours, 2 workers turned the cheese and replaced the cheesecloth with burlap. "Turning" the cheese wheel meant turning it upside down so more whey could be pressed out. The machine then pressed the cheese for 2 more hours.

WHI IMAGE ID 33272

These workers prepare to turn a wheel of cheese. It could be a 2-person job to lift these 200-pound wheels.

Casper and his crew stopped pressing and turning the cheese when no more whey drained out of it. By this time, they may have turned and pressed the cheese 3 or more times. On the last turn, they placed a special flat cheesecloth underneath so no wrinkles would form in the cheese wheel. Wrinkles could cause splits in the cheese. Mold might grow in those splits as the cheese cured.

WHI IMAGE ID 33249

Casper's workers with wheels of Swiss cheese floating in a brine tank filled with salt and water

The cheese was pressed overnight. The next morning, workers moved the cheese from the making room where temperatures often reached 110 degrees to a room where it was a cooler 55 degrees. They put the cheese wheels into a **brine** tank. A brine tank was usually about 20 feet long, 3 feet high, and about 10 feet wide. It contained salt and water.

brine: salty water

39

WHI IMAGE ID 33250

These workers take a break from washing Swiss cheese wheels. One used the low table and the other stood on the table built on a platform so he could reach the top shelves. Both tables could be rolled down the rows of curing cheese.

To prepare the brine tank, a worker added salt to the water until an egg would float in the solution. When the egg floated, he knew he had added enough salt. The salt helped form a natural cover called a "rind" on the cheese. The longer the cheese floated in the brine tank, the thicker the rind became.

After 2 or 3 days, Casper and his crew removed the cheese wheels from the brine tank. They placed the wheels on shelves in a curing room where the temperature was kept at about 75 degrees. Sometimes they stacked the heavy cheese wheels up on shelves nearly 8 feet high.

The Whole Truth about the Holes in Swiss Cheese

Do you know how the holes get in Swiss cheese?

Somebody once joked that mice ate out the holes. Can you imagine a mouse eating away at a 200-pound wheel of Swiss cheese? We know that mice like cheese, but they could never get inside such a big wheel of cheese.

Actually, nothing or nobody puts the holes in Swiss cheese. The holes or "eyes" form naturally during the curing process.

Remember the special bacterial culture that Casper added to the cheese while it was being made in the kettle? That bacterial culture causes **carbon dioxide** to form in the wheel of

This worker is cutting a wedge of Casper's Swiss cheese in the shop at his factory.

Swiss cheese after it has cured for about 3 weeks. When these bubbles of carbon dioxide gas break, they leave behind holes. Some holes are as small as a dime. Some are as large as a quarter.

Mystery solved!

carbon dioxide (**kar** buhn dye **ok** side): a gas made up of carbon and oxygen that people breathe out and plants absorb

Two or 3 times a week while the cheese was curing, Casper and his workers turned and washed the wheels of cheese with salt and whey. The washing removed any mold that had developed on the rind. Each time Casper or another worker washed a wheel of cheese, he placed it on a clean cheese lid to help prevent more mold from forming.

WHI IMAGE ID 33274

The cheese grader in the white coat inspected a piece of cheese from one of Casper's Swiss cheese wheels. He visited Casper's factory about once a week because Casper was making so much cheese! The inspector marked a grade on each wheel. The wheel also was stamped with the word "Wisconsin," the date, the wheel number, and the number given to Casper's factory.

The cheese wheels were kept in the heat cellar for 6 to 8 weeks to be cured. Casper and his workers then moved the cheese wheels to the cooler to await grading before the Swiss cheese could be sold.

Trained men called graders **inspected** each wheel of Swiss cheese. Afterward, they gave it a grade. To get a good grade, a cheese had to develop well.

The cheese grader inserted a metal tube with a sharpened end and T-shaped handle into the wheel of cheese. This tool was called a "trier." It was about 8 inches long.

A cheese trier was used to remove a core sample of cheese. It enabled the inspector to grade the wheel without cutting it open.

Once the trier was in the wheel, the grader turned it around so it would cut a core from deep inside the cheese. He removed the piece of cheese to inspect it. He looked at the size of the holes. He smelled and tasted the cheese. If the cheese did not appear to have holes or "eyes," or had only small ones, he'd say it was "blind." The grader would repeat the process at different spots. After inspecting the cheese removed from the core, the grader put the plug of cheese back into the wheel. The hole was resealed with **paraffin** so mold wouldn't form inside the wheel.

inspected (in **spek** ted): looked at very carefully
paraffin (**pa** ruh fin): a waxy substance

43

The grader gave each cheese wheel a grade of A, B, C, or D. The grade was based on the cheese's taste, appearance, and smell. If the eyes of the cheese were similar in size and larger rather than smaller, the cheese got a higher grade.

When the grader finished inspecting the cheese, he placed a mark on the wheel. The more times the grader had to put his trier into the wheel to test the cheese, the more it was marked down. Grade A was one straight mark. This was the highest grade for the best cheese. Two marks forming a T meant a grade B. Three marks forming a capital I meant a C grade. Grade-C cheese holes were too small or too large, and sometimes the cheese was missing holes. Grade-D Swiss cheese had few if any holes. The cheese grader made four marks in a number sign (#) on grade-D cheese.

The lower the grade on one of Casper's cheese wheels, the less money he could charge when selling it. But Casper had excellent cheese-making skills. He usually received the highest marks for his Swiss cheese.

Casper was truly a master cheese maker, so he had his own way of determining if the eyes were forming properly in the cheese.

He tapped the cheese wheel with his fingers in a certain way and listened for the sound. It was an art to know what he was hearing. With his experienced touch, Casper could tell how well the holes in the cheese were developing just by listening.

The longer Swiss cheese was stored or allowed to age, the sharper its flavor became. Some people preferred the taste of aged Swiss cheese. Others liked eating it before it had aged. Casper always wished his customers would wait a while after taking his cheese out of the refrigerator before they ate it. He said you could taste more of its flavor after it had some time to warm up.

"Green County Gold" was the name given to the Swiss cheese made in the area of Wisconsin that Casper called home. The name came partly from the color of the cheese. But it was also called gold because of all the money cheese makers like Casper made by selling it! That money was shared with the farmers in Green County every time a cheese maker bought their milk to make cheese. Swiss cheese was an important part of the local **economy** in Green County.

economy (ee **kahn** uh mee): the way a place runs its industry, trade, and finance

5

Life in a Cheese Factory

How would you like to get up at 4:30 every morning? That's what Casper did. He didn't have far to go to work when he made cheese at the Coldren Cheese Factory because he and Frieda and their son, Fritz, lived above it. Their living quarters included 2 bedrooms, a living room, and a kitchen.

Frieda holding Fritz. For the first few years of his life, Fritz lived with his parents right upstairs from the cheese factory where his father, Casper, worked.

Think about what it would be like to be a young boy or girl growing up in a cheese factory: the rattle of milk cans, the rich smells of fresh milk and of cheese being made, the sound of quiet conversation among workers as they turned milk into cheese. It was an exciting place. This was Fritz's world when he was a boy.

COLLECTION OF FRITZ AND DONNA JAGGI

Casper with a truck filled with his Swiss cheese. What is the name for the round objects at the right? Why does Casper have them outdoors?

When Casper loaded a truck to haul cheese to market, Fritz would put stones in his wagon to pretend he was delivering cheese, too. But kids were expected to help out as they got older. Fritz began working in the cheese factory when he was just 6 or 7 years old. He was about the age Casper was when Casper started to learn cheese making from his father in Switzerland.

"One of the first jobs I had," Fritz said, "was watching the thermometer near the copper cheese kettle as the cheese was cooking. If the temperature in the copper cheese kettle went over 40 degrees C [104 degrees F] the cheese would burn. The result would be a low-grade cheese that sold at a lesser price."

As a little boy, Fritz washed lots of cheese equipment just as Casper had done for his father. It all had to be cleaned every day. Fritz took the milk cans and whey pumps apart and washed them until they sparkled. He helped clean the stainless-steel pipes and the machine that washed the 10-gallon milk cans.

Everything had to be spotlessly clean in a cheese factory. State inspectors would come by without warning to make sure everything was in tip-top shape. Casper was proud of his factory. He called it a "100 percent plant." This was because he always passed state inspections with a 100 percent perfect score for cleanliness.

These freshly washed milk cans would be returned to the farmers for refilling when Casper's 6 trucks went out to pick up more milk. How many cans can you count in this picture?

As Fritz got older and stronger, he had the job of "intake" man. This meant he dumped the cans of milk into the scale tank as the milk hauler unloaded them.

A gallon of milk weighed about 8.6 pounds. So 10 gallons of milk weighed 86 pounds. Add the weight of the metal milk can (15 pounds or so), and a can of fresh milk weighed a total of more than 100 pounds! Can you lift 100 pounds? It's not easy. When the milk cans were empty, Fritz pushed them into the can washer to get them ready to be sent back to the farmer. Then the farmer could fill them once again.

49

Dumping cans of milk, one after the other, day after day doesn't sound very exciting. But interesting things happened at the cheese factory. For instance, one farmer had been complaining to Casper that his milk's butterfat content was testing low.

Casper asked the farmer, "Is your wife taking cream out of your milk cans to use for baking?"

"No, no," the farmer answered. "She wouldn't do that."

Fritz had noticed something of interest while dumping the milk from the farmer's cans into the cheese factory's scale tank. "Come inside for a minute," Fritz said to the farmer. "I want to show you something."

The farmer walked into the factory intake room.

"Does this coffee cup look familiar?" Fritz asked. "Would this coffee cup belong to your wife's china set?"

"Well, this cup does look familiar," the farmer said with a **sheepish** grin on his face.

"It came out of your milk can!" Fritz said. "Your wife must have dropped it in the can when she was skimming cream."

That answered the question of why the farmer's milk had so little butterfat!

Many farmers' wives skimmed cream from the milk, especially on holidays and weekends when they wanted fresh cream. Casper decided not to test his farmers' milk on holidays and weekends because he knew the results would be lower than the rest of the week.

Casper's milk haulers picked up milk from 145 farmers. Each truck left the cheese factory by 7:00 a.m. to make its rounds. When Fritz was old enough to get a driver's license, he drove one of his father's milk trucks.

sheepish: showing embarrassment when you realize you are at fault

51

Fritz usually returned to the factory with his last load of milk by 11:00 a.m. Once a worker finished his second milk run, he helped with the cheese making. The sooner the milk arrived at the factory, the quicker it could be made into cheese, and the sooner the men could go home.

Winter could be difficult for the milk truck drivers. Snowplows did not keep the highways clear back in the 1940s and 1950s as they do today. The milk truck drivers working for Casper took along a second man with a shovel.

Fritz remembers one time when a milk truck ran out of gas. He took 5 gallons of gasoline out to the truck and poured the fuel into the truck's gasoline tank. Then he tossed the empty gasoline can into the back of the truck with the cans of fresh milk.

"I found out that you don't do that," Fritz said. "We had to throw away 50 cans of milk because they had picked up the gasoline smell."

Young Fritz was not above pulling pranks at the cheese factory. Around the Fourth of July one year, he lit a firecracker that rolled underneath one of the tanks. It was a big firecracker, and when it went off, the shaking knocked a ceiling light into a cheese kettle. Glass shattered in the near-empty kettle. Fritz didn't toss firecrackers into the cheese factory again.

Frieda took Fritz and Annabelle to church every Sunday morning. Casper stayed behind at the cheese factory because he had no days off. Sometimes on Sundays, when the cheese making was finished a little early, the Jaggi family would visit relatives or head to New Glarus for Swiss entertainment. When he had free time, Casper also liked to play the accordion. In winter, when things weren't quite as busy as in summer, he went bowling with friends. But there was not much time for doing things other than work at the factory.

Fritz and his sister, Annabelle. He wore traditional Swiss clothing to attend a local festival.

Casper and his workers even made cheese on Christmas Day, since cows needed to be milked on holidays, too!

Working in the cheese factory was a series of activities that went on day after day. The milk trucks made the rounds of the farms, picking up the milk and delivering it to the cheese factory. Workers dumped cans of fresh milk into a scale tank until there was enough to fill one kettle. Casper would supervise the making of the milk into Swiss cheese. By midafternoon, the crew had completed the day's work except for cleanup. They'd wash equipment and get things ready for the next day's operation. They'd crawl out of bed by 4:30 the next morning to repeat it all once more.

Thousands of pounds of Swiss cheese resulted from all the hard work. People across the country enjoyed the cheese Casper and workers like Fritz made at the Brodhead Swiss Cheese Factory. These customers liked its fresh, nutty taste and the holes that made it **distinctive**. Although Fritz did not continue as a cheese maker when Casper retired, he enjoyed learning the craft of cheese making from his father.

distinctive (dis **tingk** tiv): easy to identify

6

The Cheddar Cheese Challenge

By the early 1950s, the market for Swiss cheese had started to **decline**. Many families preferred a different kind of cheese. Often this meant a milder-tasting cheese. With less demand for Swiss cheese, many Green County factories closed. Some factories switched to making cheddar, mozzarella, and other types of cheese.

Casper realized he needed another product to stay in business. Cheddar cheese was, and still is, the most popular cheese made in Wisconsin. Casper decided to add cheddar making to his cheese factory to attract more customers. Cheddar did not take as long to cure as Swiss cheese, so it could be sold more quickly and didn't need to be stored as long. That would be good for business, too.

decline (dee **kline**): to get smaller, less important, or worse

WHI IMAGE ID 33392

Casper used stainless-steel vats like these for making cheddar cheese. He used the round copper kettles only for his Swiss cheese.

Making cheddar cheese is also a very different process from making Swiss.

Casper made cheddar cheese by pouring milk into long stainless-steel vats instead of the round copper kettles used for his Swiss. He added a bacterial culture, but it was not the same one added to Swiss. Casper also added a coloring agent to make his cheddar cheese slightly orange. The coloring agent is called "**annatto**." Annatto is a natural vegetable dye made from annatto seeds. Casper then added rennet to the vat, which caused curds to form. As you'll remember, he used rennet in his Swiss cheese, too.

annatto (uh **nah** toe)

Cheddar curds began to form as big mechanical arms automatically stirred the milk for about 30 minutes. When the milk was the same thickness as pudding, Casper and his workers pulled wire knives through the vat from one end to the other, and back and forth. The wire knives cut the **coagulated** milk into cubes. Remember that when Casper made Swiss cheese, he used a cheese harp instead.

Next, Casper gently heated the cheddar curds to 103 degrees. That was about 20 degrees lower than the temperature he used for his Swiss cheese curds. He drained the whey by opening a valve at the bottom of the vat. Remember that when Casper made Swiss cheese, he removed the bag of curds from the cheese kettle, leaving behind the whey.

At this stage in making his cheddar cheese, Casper added salt to the cheddar curds. The salt slowed down the bacterial culture and the formation of lactic acid. Without the salt, the curds would crumble and Casper wouldn't be able to press them together to form the cheese.

coagulated (koh **ag** yoo lay ted): thickened or gathered into a mass

As the whey was drained out of the vat, the pressure caused the cheddar curds to mat together. Curds filled the entire length of the vat. Casper and his workers cut the curds into 18-inch-long loaves. After about 30 minutes, the loaves were firm enough to be turned. Casper and his work team turned the loaves several times to remove as much whey as possible. "Cheddaring" is the name given to turning the loaves. It's also where cheddar cheese got its name. Next, Casper ran the loaves through a cheddaring machine to cut the loaves into small chunks of curd. For many people, eating these fresh curds is a special treat. When you bite into a fresh curd, the cheese squeaks. That's how you know the curd is fresh! And it's part of the fun of eating fresh cheese curds.

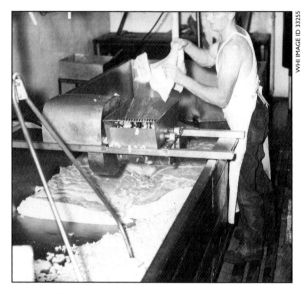

WHI IMAGE ID 33255

One of Casper's workers runs loaves of cheddar cheese through a cheddar mill. The machine cuts the loaves into small curds.

Casper and his crew scooped the small chunks of cheddar curd into buckets and dumped them into metal forms. They pressed these forms to remove any remaining whey. This step also shaped the curds into a smooth piece of cheddar cheese. When making Swiss cheese, Casper pressed the

WHI IMAGE ID 33255

In this picture, the photographer focused on the rectangular cheddar cheese forms instead of the people. Casper and his workers lined these metal forms with cheesecloth before pressing the cheese.

curd into the shape of a big wheel. But for his cheddar cheese, Casper pressed the curd into a rectangular shape. Casper pressed his Swiss cheese into 200-pound wheels. His cheddar was pressed into 40-pound blocks.

Cheddar is cured at a lower temperature than Swiss cheese. Casper aged the cheddar in the curing room at 40 degrees. Just as with Swiss cheese, the longer cheddar cheese aged, the sharper and stronger the flavor. Casper aged some of his cheddar cheese for 3 years. The longer cheese ages, the more expensive it is to buy.

7

A Lifetime Spent Perfecting His Craft

Casper ran his
Brodhead Swiss Cheese
Factory until 1958, when
he retired. He was having
health problems, so he and
Frieda moved to Tucson,
Arizona. They thought
the climate there would
be better for him. They
had been married nearly
50 years when Casper
died on January 20,
1971. He was 77. Frieda
returned to Wisconsin and
lived until she was 98.

We Extend Our Congratulations To Brodhead On Its 100th Birthday

Since 1940 the Brodhead Swiss Cheese factory, the largest in Wisconsin, has been proud to be a part of the community.

To our many faithful employees, the company would like to take this opportunity to express its gratitude. They have worked hand- in-hand with the management to make the finest Swiss and American cheese.

To our many farmer friends who supply the milk, we say "thank you". Your continued co-operation is always encouraging.

OUR SINCERE BEST WISHES TO ALL.

Brodhead Swiss Cheese Factory

CASPER JAGGI

Casper placed this announcement in the Brodhead newspaper in 1956. What does this tell you about his relationship with local farmers?

WHI IMAGE ID 33279

Casper had local artist Frank Engebretson paint this scene of the Swiss Alps onto the side of his Brodhead Swiss Cheese Factory. It represents Casper's love for his homeland and Switzerland's tradition of cheese making.

Their son, Fritz, and daughter, Annabelle, are both still in Wisconsin. Fritz and his wife, Donna, raised their family and live just a few blocks from where his father's factory was located.

As a 20-year-old European immigrant, Casper Jaggi arrived in a strange land. He brought with him an understanding of cheese making, which his father had taught him in the Swiss Alps when he was a young boy. Casper did other work when he first arrived in the United States, but his love for making cheese continued throughout his lifetime.

For Casper, cheese making was an art that he perfected over many years.

While running his business, Casper never forgot his father's words: "If you can't do a job right, don't do it at all." If you asked Casper's many loyal workers and customers about how he did his job, they would say he was a **perfectionist**.

© 2007 WISCONSIN MILK MARKETING BOARD INC.

Thousands of designs were submitted for the Wisconsin quarter. As you can see, the winner contains symbols of our state's agricultural heritage— including a cow and the cheese made from its milk!

Casper was one of the cheese-making pioneers who came to Wisconsin from Switzerland. Along with other cheese makers, he helped establish a tradition that made Wisconsin known throughout the world as a cheese-making state. The tradition continues today.

Casper Jaggi was clearly a master cheese maker. He set a fine example for those cheese makers who followed him. In 1994, Wisconsin created a special program to train and certify

perfectionist (pur **fek** shun ist): a person who works hard to make something the best it can possibly be

master cheese makers. People applying for the program must have at least 10 years' experience and be an active licensed Wisconsin cheese maker.

Wisconsin cheese makers have also established the Wisconsin Dairy **Artisan** Network. These artisan cheese makers pride themselves in producing handcrafted cheese made in small batches. Some of these cheese makers even use milk from cows, goats, and sheep they raise themselves.

Today, Wisconsin cheese makers compete against cheese makers from other states and countries. Wisconsin's cheeses win many national and international awards. Cheese making continues to be a delicious part of Wisconsin's heritage.

COLLECTION OF HOLLAND'S FAMILY FARM

These twin girls are the next generation of Wisconsin cheese makers. Their parents, Rolf and Marieke Penterman, immigrated to Wisconsin from Holland. In 2002, the Pentermans started turning their cows' milk into Gouda, a traditional Dutch cheese. Their farm in Thorp is called Holland's Family Farm.

artisan (ahr tuh **zahn**): a person who produces something in small amounts using traditional methods

63

8

A Tradition Continues

In the late 1800s, Green County quickly became a major cheese-making area in the United States. In 1885, Green County produced 3.2 million pounds of cheese. By the mid-1940s, the county's cheese production had increased to more than 18 million pounds per year. By 1973, Green County was producing 36 million pounds of cheese annually. That's a lot of cheese.

During much of the early 1900s, Green County was famous for its Swiss cheese. Slowly, the county's cheese makers began switching to other kinds of cheese making. Swiss cheese started to be made in blocks instead of the big wheels, which made it similar to cheddar and many other cheeses. Customers thought it was easier to cut blocks of cheese for their sandwiches.

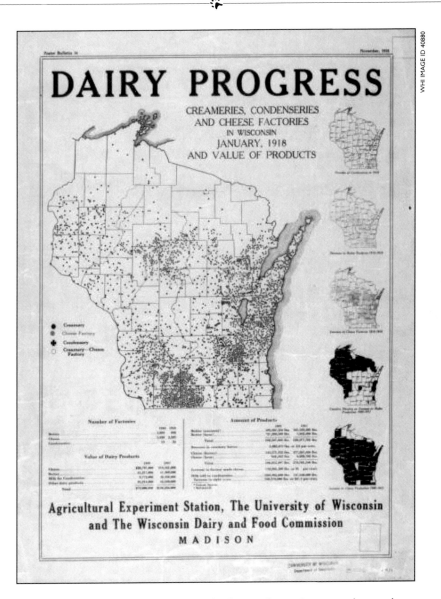

This map shows where Wisconsin's cheese factories were located in 1918. Can you name the 2 counties that had the most cheese factories back then? Why do they look familiar?

In 2007, there were 13 cheese factories operating in Green County. They have interesting names, such as Chalet Cheese Co-op, Maple Leaf Cheese Factory, Klondike, Edelweiss Creamery, Deppeler Cheese Factory, Decatur Dairy, and Roth Käse. They produce many thousands of pounds of cheese each year. They make many different kinds of cheese: **Colby**, cheddar, **Havarti**, **Muenster**, Butterkase, Monterey Jack, Edam, **Gouda**, Swiss, and Limburger. Just 4 cheese factories in Green County still make Swiss cheese. Only one of those makes it the old-fashioned way in large cheese wheels, as Casper Jaggi did.

There have been many changes in dairy farming in Green County, where Casper once worked as a cheese maker. Even though Green County still produces a lot of cheese, the numbers of dairy farms and milk cows are getting smaller. In 1975, there were 1,142 dairy farms in the county. By 2004, the number had dropped to 406. In 1980, there were 50,200 dairy cows grazing the sweeping hills of Green County. By 2006, the number of cows had declined to 31,000.

Colby (**kohl** be)
Havarti (hah **var** tee)
Muenster (**mun** stur)
Gouda (**goo** dah)

Some of the 500 styles and types of cheeses produced in Wisconsin today

While there are fewer dairy farmers across the rest of the state, too, Wisconsin still uses the milk from farmers' cows to make about 2.4 billion pounds of cheese a year. Wisconsin is a national leader in the production of cheese and prides itself in making quality cheese. Wisconsin is the only state in the nation that requires a licensed cheese maker to oversee the production of every pound of cheese. In 2007, the state had 1,222 active licensed cheese makers.

Did You Know?

Today, 90 percent of Wisconsin's milk becomes cheese.

Appendix

Casper's Time Line

mid-1820s — First Swiss immigrants come to Wisconsin.

1845 — The first Swiss settlement is established in New Glarus, Wisconsin, by Nicholas Durst and Fridolin Steiff.

1893 — Casper is born on August 13.

1899 — Casper's father starts teaching him about making Swiss cheese.

1913 — Casper, age 20, follows his brothers to New Glarus. He starts helping them clear farm fields but discovers he misses making cheese.

1920 — Casper meets Frieda Fuhrer, another Swiss immigrant.

February 21, 1921 — Casper and Frieda get married.

1923 — Casper and Frieda move to northeastern Wisconsin so Casper can work at Kraft Foods company in Antigo.

1924 — Casper and Frieda return to Green County. He gets a job making cheese at County Line Factory near Albany.

1925–1940 — Casper works at Coldren Cheese Factory near Brodhead. He and Frieda live above the factory.

1938 — Casper and Frieda adopt their son, Fritz.

1941 — Casper buys his own cheese factory in Brodhead. He calls it the Brodhead Swiss Cheese Factory.

1943 — Casper and Frieda adopt their daughter, Annabelle.

1950s — Casper's factory becomes the largest Swiss cheese factory in Wisconsin. During this time, Swiss cheese becomes less popular. Casper decides to start making cheddar cheese, too.

1958 — Casper retires. He and Frieda move to Tucson, Arizona.

1971 — Casper dies on January 20 at age 77.

2007 — There are 13 cheese factories in Green County. Just 4 of them still make Swiss cheese, and only one sells it in large cheese wheels, as Casper did.

Glossary

acidity (ah **si** duh tee): the amount of acid and sourness something contains

acre (**ay** kur): a measurement of area that is almost the size of a football field

appealing: pleasing and of interest

art: a skill gained after much practice and study

artisan (ahr tuh **zahn**): a person who produces something in small amounts using traditional methods

bacteria (bak **teer** ee uh): microscopic living things all around you and inside you

brine: salty water

by-product: something that is left over after you make or do something

canton: one of the states of Switzerland

carbon dioxide (**kar** buhn dye **ok** side): a gas made up of carbon and oxygen that people breathe out and plants absorb

cheese harp: a tool with a wooden frame and thin wires that is used to cut curds of cheese

coagulated (koh **ag** yoo lay ted): thickened or gathered into a mass

consistency (kuhn **siss** tuhn see): degree of firmness

conveyor belt (kuhn **vay** ur belt): a moving belt that brings items to different places in a factory

cooperative (koh **op** ur uh tiv): a business owned by all the people who work in it or are members of it

cream separator: a machine for separating cream from milk

culture (**kuhl** chur): a living material grown in a prepared medium

curd (**kurd**): the solid part of sour milk that is used to make cheese

cured (**kyurd**): prepared for use

decline (dee **kline**): to get smaller, less important, or worse

demonstration: a display of how something is done

diameter: a straight line from one side of a circle, through the center, and to the other side

distinctive (dis **tingk** tiv): easy to identify

drove: moved something in a certain direction

economy (ee **kahn** uh mee): the way a place runs its industry, trade, and finance

edible (**ed** uh buhl): able to be eaten

employee: someone who works for another and receives a salary from that person or business

entrepreneur (ahn truh preh **nur**): person who starts his or her business from scratch

expert: someone who knows a lot about a topic

form: a frame or mold that will give something a particular shape

frustrated: to feel helpless and discouraged

grazing: feeding on grass growing in a field

heritage (**her** uh tij): traditions and culture passed on
  by ancestors

highland: an area with mountains or hills

immigrant (**im** uh gruhnt): someone who leaves a country
  to permanently live in another country

imported: brought into a country from another place
  or region

inexpensive: reasonable in price

innovative: known for new ideas or new inventions

inspected (in **spek** ted): looked at very carefully

lactose (lak **tos**): a sugar that is present in milk

manager: person in charge of a business or other employees
  at work

master: an expert

mechanize (**meh** ka nize): to use machinery to replace
  human or animal labor

milligram: a unit of measurement in the metric system

mold: a fungus that grows on old food or damp surfaces

nutrient (**noo** tree uhnt): something that is needed to stay healthy

ounce: a unit of weight equal to 1/16 of a pound

palate (**pal** it): a person's sense of taste

paraffin (**pa** ruh fin): a waxy substance

percentage (pur **sen** tij): a portion of the whole amount

perfectionist (pur **fek** shun ist): a person who works hard to make something the best it can possibly be

perishable (**per** ish uh buhl): likely to spoil or decay

plant: a factory where a particular product is made

rennet (**re** nuht): an enzyme, or complex protein, added to milk to cause it to start changing from a liquid to a solid form.

sharpened: improved

sheepish: showing embarrassment when you realize you are at fault

spur: a railroad track that branches off from the main line

strenuous (**stren** yoo uhss): needing great effort

symbol: a design or object that is a representation of
something else

till: to prepare land for growing crops

tuffet: a low seat or stool

whey (**way**): the watery part of milk that separates in sour
milk or when you make cheese

wholesaler: someone who buys large amounts of a product
at a lower price in order to resell it at a higher price

yield (**yeeld**): to produce something

Reading Group Guide and Activities

Discussion Questions

- Casper came to the United States with very little money. He eventually started a company and worked long and hard until his Swiss cheese factory became the biggest one in Wisconsin. Name 3 things that made Casper a successful businessman. How did these things help him become successful?

- When Casper was working at the Coldren Cheese Factory, he, his wife, Frieda, and their young son, Fritz, lived right upstairs. Do you think you'd like to live so close to where your mother or father works? What would be the advantages? What would be the difficulties?

- The photos in this book add to a reader's understanding of how cow's milk was made into Swiss cheese at Casper's factory. Which photo told you the most about Casper's life and work? Explain what you learned from that image.

- Have you heard the saying, "Don't put all your eggs in one basket"? After you read chapter 6, think about those words. Do you think Casper followed this advice? If so, what did he do? Can you think of an example of a time in your life when you didn't put all your eggs in one basket?

Activities

❧ Casper's father taught him about cheese making. What crafts, skills, or traditions have your parents or grandparents passed on to you? Teach your friends how to do one of those things you've learned from a relative.

❧ Host a Swiss cheese-tasting test. Have a paper and pencil for each cheese taster. Buy 3 different kinds of Swiss cheese. Try to find one from Green County or elsewhere in Wisconsin, one from another part of the United States, and one from Switzerland. Cut up the cheese and keep the 3 types separate. Only one person should know which cheese is which! Take a sample of the first cheese and write down what you think about it. What does it taste like? What does it smell like? Does it remind you of anything else? Take a look at the holes. If you were a cheese grader like the man who visited Casper's factory, what grade would you give it? Before sampling the next one, eat a cracker to clear your **palate**. After your friends or classmates have tried all 3 and written down their opinions of each, it's time to find out which cheese is from which location. Were they surprised to discover where their favorite Swiss cheese was made?

❧ The idea for this book came from Casper's son, Fritz. He shared many of the photos you see in this book with Bobbie Malone of the Wisconsin Historical Society Press. Then the author, Jerry Apps, interviewed Fritz to ask him about his father's life. If you were going to tell the story of one of your family members, whose would you tell? Interview that person and then write up an outline of the book you'd like a publisher to print. What do you think will make your relative's story interesting to readers?

palate (**pal** it): a person's sense of taste

To Learn More about Cheese Making in Wisconsin

Online Sources

Babcock Hall Dairy Plant, University of Wisconsin–Madison
http://foodsci.wisc.edu/store: This campus cheese factory also bottles milk and makes yogurt and ice cream. You can tour the factory and buy Babcock cheese, ice cream, and other dairy products at its retail store.

Wisconsin Cheese Factories and Tours
www.wisconline.com/attractions/cheese.html: Here you'll find a list of working Wisconsin cheese factories and tour information.

Wisconsin Dairy Artisan Network
www.wisconsindairyartisan.org: This Web site includes details about artisan and farmstead cheeses. It also offers tips on storing and serving different types of cheese.

Wisconsin Department of Agriculture, Trade and Consumer Protection
www.datcp.state.wi.us: This site has information about dairy farming, cows, cheese, and more.

Wisconsin Milk Marketing Board
www.wisdairy.com: Games and activities for kids, plus information about the state's history of cheese making, dairy farming, and different types of cheese are on this Web site.

Wisconsin Cheese Museums and Sites to Visit

1867 Bodenstab Cheese Factory Museum, Sheboygan County Historical Society Museum: Displays include early-nineteenth-century cheese-making equipment. 3110 Erie Avenue, Sheboygan; (920) 458-1103; www.co.sheboygan.wi.us/html/d_museum.html.

Heritage Hill: This state historic park includes an 1894 cheese factory. 2640 S. Webster Avenue, Green Bay; (920) 448-5150; www.heritagehillgb.org.

Historic Cheesemaking Center: The displays include Swiss cheese kettles and cheese-making equipment used for making Swiss and Limburger cheeses. You can watch videotapes of cheese makers, milk haulers, and cheese dealers who once worked in southern Wisconsin. 2108 Seventh Avenue, Monroe; (608) 325-4636.

Stonefield: This Wisconsin historic site has a replica of an 1890 Wisconsin cheese factory complete with cheese vats, presses, and a butterfat milk tester. Off Highway 133 on County Road VV, Cassville; (608) 725-5210; www.wisconsinhistory.org/stonefield.

Swiss Historical Village and Museum: One of the 14 buildings here is a replica of a cheese factory with 100-year-old cheese-making equipment, including a copper kettle used for making Swiss cheese. 612 Seventh Avenue, New Glarus; (608) 527-2317; www.swisshistoricalvillage.org.

Acknowledgments

Fritz Jaggi, Casper Jaggi's son, was of special help for this book. He provided most of the photos and shared his memories of his father's cheese-making career. He also read portions of the manuscript, suggested changes, and patiently answered my unending questions.

Bobbie Malone, director of the Office of School Services at the Wisconsin Historical Society, and Erica Schock, former publications editor at the Wisconsin Historical Society Press, initially interviewed Fritz and obtained valuable information for this story. Bobbie was also of great assistance in helping me work through several revisions of the work. Laura Kearney, editor, Wisconsin Historical Society Press, worked long and hard to make this book easily accessible to young readers, as well as accurate in every way possible.

Susan Apps Horman, my daughter and a sixth-grade teacher at Sherman Middle School in Madison, Wisconsin, read the manuscript several times and offered many suggestions on how to make the material young-adult friendly.

My wife, Ruth, who reads all of my manuscripts with a careful eye and a critical touch, was once more of invaluable assistance.

Index

This index points you to the pages where you can read about persons, places, and ideas. If you do not find the word you are looking for, try to think of another word that means about the same thing.

When you see a page number in **bold** it means there is a picture on that page.